TABLE OF RECIPES

Cooking is like love.
It should be entered into with
abandon or not at all.
HARRIET VAN HORNE

TABLE OF RECIPES

#	RECIPE NAME	NOTES
1		
2		
3		
4		
5		
6		
7		
8		
9		
10		
11		
12		
13		
14		
15		
16		
17		
18		
19		
20		
21		
22		
23		
24		
25		

Always start out with a larger pot than what you think you need.

TABLE OF RECIPES

#	RECIPE NAME	NOTES
26		
27		
28		
29		
30		
31		
32		
33		
34		
35		
36		
37		
38		
39		
40		
41		
42		
43		
44		
45		
46		
47		
48		
49		
50		

Laughter is brightest in the place where the food is.
IRISH PROVERB

TABLE OF RECIPES

#	RECIPE NAME	NOTES
51		
52		
53		
54		
55		
56		
57		
58		
59		
60		
61		
62		
63		
64		
65		
66		
67		
68		
69		
70		
71		
72		
73		
74		
75		

The only real stumbling block is fear of failure.
In cooking you've got to have a what-the-hell attitude.

TABLE OF RECIPES

#	RECIPE NAME	NOTES
76		
77		
78		
79		
80		
81		
82		
83		
84		
85		
86		
87		
88		
89		
90		
91		
92		
93		
94		
95		
96		
97		
98		
99		
100		

Too many cooks spoil the broth.
CHINESE PROVERB

CONVERSION TABLES

Always start out with a larger pot than
what you think you need.
JULIA CHILD

MEASURE EQUIVALENTS

1 tablespoon (tbsp)	=	3 teaspoons (tsp)
1/16 cup (c)	=	1 tablespoon (tbsp)
1/6 cup	=	2 tablespoons + 2 tsp
1/4 cup	=	4 tablespoons
1/3 cup	=	5 tablespoons + 1 tsp
3/8 cup	=	6 tablespoons
1/2 cup	=	8 tablespoons
2/3 cup	=	10 tablespoons + 2 tsp
1 cup	=	16 tbsp (or 48 tsp)
8 fluid ounces (fl oz)	=	1 cup
1 pint (pt)	=	2 cups
1 quart (qt)	=	2 pints
4 cups	=	1 quart
1 gallon (gal)	=	4 quarts
16 ounces (oz)	=	1 pound (lb)
1 milliliter (mL)	=	1 cubic centimeter (cc)
1 inch (in)	=	2.54 centimeters (cm)

VOLUME CONVERSION (Dry)

1/8 teaspoon	=	0.5 mL
1/4 teaspoon	=	1 mL
1/2 teaspoon	=	2 mL
3/4 teaspoon	=	4 mL
1 teaspoon	=	5 mL
1 tablespoon	=	15 mL
2 tablespoons	=	30 mL
3 tablespoons	=	45 mL
1/4 cup	=	60 mL
1/3 cup	=	75 mL
1/2 cup	=	125 mL
2/3 cup	=	150 mL
3/4 cup	=	175 mL
1 cup	=	250 mL
2 cups (1 pint)	=	500 mL
3 cups	=	750 mL
4 cups (1 quart)	=	1 L

VOLUME CONVERSION (Fluid)

1 fluid ounce (2 tbsp)	=	30 mL
4 fluid ounces (1/2 cup)	=	125 mL
8 fluid ounces (1 cup)	=	250 mL
12 fluid ounces (1.5 cups)	=	375 mL
16 fluid ounces (2 cups)	=	500 mL

TEMP CONVERSION (Oven)

250°F	=	120°C
300°F	=	150°C
350°F	=	180°C
400°F	=	200°C
450°F	=	230°C

You don't have to be a chef or even a particularly good cook to experience proper kitchen alchemy: the moment when ingredients combine to form something more delectable than the sum of their parts.

ERIN MORGENSTERN

METRIC CONVERSION FACTORS (Mass and Volume)

MULTIPLY	BY	TO GET
Fluid Ounces	29.57	grams
Ounces (dry)	28.35	grams
Grams	0.0353	ounces
Grams	0.0022	pounds
Kilograms	2.21	pounds
Pounds	453.6	grams
Pounds	0.4536	kilograms
Quarts	0.946	liters
Quarts (dry)	67.2	cubic inches
Quarts (liquid)	57.7	cubic inches
Liters	1.0567	quarts
Gallons	3,785	cubic centimeters
Gallons	3.785	liters

MASS CONVERSION

1/2 ounce	=	14 g
1 ounce	=	28 g
4 ounces	=	115 g
8 ounces	=	230 g
10 ounces	=	280 g
12 ounces	=	340 g
16 ounces (1 lb)	=	450 g

LENGTH CONVERSION

1/16 inch	=	1.5 mm
1/8 inch	=	3 mm
1/4 inch	=	6 mm
1/2 inch	=	1.2 cm
3/4 inch	=	2 cm
1 inch	=	2.5 cm
1 foot	=	0.3 m

Too many cooks spoil the broth.
CHINESE PROVERB

ESTIMATED DAILY CALORIE NEEDS - Female

Age	CALORIE RANGE	
	Sedentary	Active
2 to 3 years	1,000	1,400
4 to 8	1,200	1,800
9 to 13	1,600	2,200
14 to 18	1,800	2,400
19 to 30	2,000	2,400
31 to 50	1,800	2,200
51+	1,600	2,200

ESTIMATED DAILY CALORIE NEEDS - Male

Age	CALORIE RANGE	
	Sedentary	Active
2 to 3 years	1,000	1,400
4 to 8	1,400	2,000
9 to 13	1,800	2,600
14 to 18	2,200	3,200
19 to 30	2,400	3,000
31 to 50	2,200	3,000
51+	2,000	2,800

The shared meal is no small thing. It is a foundation of family life, the place where our children learn the art of conversation and acquire the habits of civilization: sharing, listening, taking turns, navigating differences, arguing without offending. What have been called the "cultural contradictions of capitalism"—its tendency to undermine the stabilizing social forms it depends on—are on vivid display today at the modern American dinner table, along with all the brightly colored packages that the food industry has managed to plant there.

MICHAEL POLLAN

RECIPES

For is there any practice less selfish,
any labour less alienated, any time less
wasted, than preparing something delicious and
nourishing for people you love?
MICHAEL POLLAN

01 RECIPE:

SERVES	PREPARATION TIME	COOK TIME	DATE

DIRECTIONS

INGREDIENTS

NOTES:

02  RECIPE:

SERVES	PREPARATION TIME	COOK TIME	DATE

DIRECTIONS

INGREDIENTS

NOTES:

03  RECIPE:

| SERVES | PREPARATION TIME | COOK TIME | DATE |

DIRECTIONS

INGREDIENTS

NOTES:

04  RECIPE:

| SERVES | PREPARATION TIME | COOK TIME | DATE |

DIRECTIONS

INGREDIENTS

NOTES:

05

RECIPE:

| SERVES | PREPARATION TIME | COOK TIME | DATE |

DIRECTIONS

INGREDIENTS

NOTES:

06  RECIPE:

| SERVES | PREPARATION TIME | COOK TIME | DATE |

DIRECTIONS

INGREDIENTS

NOTES:

07  RECIPE:

SERVES

PREPARATION TIME

COOK TIME

DATE

DIRECTIONS

INGREDIENTS

NOTES:

08

RECIPE:

SERVES

PREPARATION TIME

COOK TIME

DATE

DIRECTIONS

INGREDIENTS

NOTES:

09  RECIPE:

| SERVES | PREPARATION TIME | COOK TIME | DATE |

DIRECTIONS

INGREDIENTS

NOTES:

RECIPE:

SERVES

PREPARATION TIME

COOK TIME

DATE

DIRECTIONS

INGREDIENTS

NOTES:

RECIPE:

SERVES	PREPARATION TIME	COOK TIME	DATE

DIRECTIONS

INGREDIENTS

NOTES:

RECIPE:

| SERVES | PREPARATION TIME | COOK TIME | DATE |

DIRECTIONS

INGREDIENTS

NOTES:

13  RECIPE:

SERVES

PREPARATION TIME

COOK TIME

DATE

DIRECTIONS

INGREDIENTS

NOTES:

RECIPE:

SERVES	PREPARATION TIME	COOK TIME	DATE

DIRECTIONS

INGREDIENTS

NOTES:

15

RECIPE:

SERVES

PREPARATION TIME

COOK TIME

DATE

DIRECTIONS

INGREDIENTS

NOTES:

16  RECIPE:

SERVES | **PREPARATION TIME** | **COOK TIME** | **DATE**

DIRECTIONS

INGREDIENTS

NOTES:

17

RECIPE:

| SERVES | PREPARATION TIME | COOK TIME | DATE |

DIRECTIONS

INGREDIENTS

NOTES:

RECIPE:

| SERVES | PREPARATION TIME | COOK TIME | DATE |

DIRECTIONS

INGREDIENTS

NOTES:

19  RECIPE:

SERVES

PREPARATION TIME

COOK TIME

DATE

DIRECTIONS

INGREDIENTS

NOTES:

20

RECIPE:

| SERVES | PREPARATION TIME | COOK TIME | DATE |

DIRECTIONS

INGREDIENTS

NOTES:

RECIPE:

| SERVES | PREPARATION TIME | COOK TIME | DATE |

DIRECTIONS

INGREDIENTS

NOTES:

RECIPE:

SERVES

PREPARATION TIME

COOK TIME

DATE

DIRECTIONS

INGREDIENTS

NOTES:

RECIPE:

SERVES | **PREPARATION TIME** | **COOK TIME** | **DATE**

DIRECTIONS

INGREDIENTS

NOTES:

RECIPE:

SERVES

PREPARATION TIME

COOK TIME

DATE

DIRECTIONS

INGREDIENTS

NOTES:

25

RECIPE:

SERVES

PREPARATION TIME

COOK TIME

DATE

DIRECTIONS

INGREDIENTS

NOTES:

RECIPE:

SERVES

PREPARATION TIME

COOK TIME

DATE

DIRECTIONS

INGREDIENTS

NOTES:

RECIPE:

SERVES

PREPARATION TIME

COOK TIME

DATE

DIRECTIONS

INGREDIENTS

NOTES:

RECIPE:

| SERVES | PREPARATION TIME | COOK TIME | DATE |

DIRECTIONS

INGREDIENTS

NOTES:

29

RECIPE:

| SERVES | PREPARATION TIME | COOK TIME | DATE |

DIRECTIONS

INGREDIENTS

NOTES:

30  RECIPE:

SERVES

PREPARATION TIME

COOK TIME

DATE

DIRECTIONS

INGREDIENTS

NOTES:

RECIPE:

SERVES	PREPARATION TIME	COOK TIME	DATE

DIRECTIONS

INGREDIENTS

NOTES:

RECIPE:

| SERVES | PREPARATION TIME | COOK TIME | DATE |

DIRECTIONS

INGREDIENTS

NOTES:

33

RECIPE:

SERVES	PREPARATION TIME	COOK TIME	DATE

DIRECTIONS

INGREDIENTS

NOTES:

RECIPE:

| SERVES | PREPARATION TIME | COOK TIME | DATE |

DIRECTIONS

INGREDIENTS

NOTES:

RECIPE:

SERVES | **PREPARATION TIME** | **COOK TIME** | **DATE**

DIRECTIONS

INGREDIENTS

NOTES:

RECIPE:

SERVES	PREPARATION TIME	COOK TIME	DATE

DIRECTIONS

INGREDIENTS

NOTES:

37

RECIPE:

| SERVES | PREPARATION TIME | COOK TIME | DATE |

DIRECTIONS

INGREDIENTS

NOTES:

RECIPE:

| SERVES | PREPARATION TIME | COOK TIME | DATE |

DIRECTIONS

INGREDIENTS

NOTES:

RECIPE:

SERVES	PREPARATION TIME	COOK TIME	DATE

DIRECTIONS

INGREDIENTS

NOTES:

RECIPE:

SERVES

PREPARATION TIME

COOK TIME

DATE

DIRECTIONS

INGREDIENTS

NOTES:

RECIPE:

| SERVES | PREPARATION TIME | COOK TIME | DATE |

DIRECTIONS

INGREDIENTS

NOTES:

42

RECIPE:

SERVES

PREPARATION TIME

COOK TIME

DATE

DIRECTIONS

INGREDIENTS

NOTES:

RECIPE:

SERVES	PREPARATION TIME	COOK TIME	DATE

DIRECTIONS

INGREDIENTS

NOTES:

RECIPE:

SERVES

PREPARATION TIME

COOK TIME

DATE

DIRECTIONS

INGREDIENTS

NOTES:

45  RECIPE:

| SERVES | PREPARATION TIME | COOK TIME | DATE |

DIRECTIONS

INGREDIENTS

NOTES:

RECIPE:

SERVES	PREPARATION TIME	COOK TIME	DATE

DIRECTIONS

INGREDIENTS

NOTES:

RECIPE:

SERVES	PREPARATION TIME	COOK TIME	DATE

DIRECTIONS

INGREDIENTS

NOTES:

RECIPE:

SERVES | **PREPARATION TIME** | **COOK TIME** | **DATE**

DIRECTIONS | **INGREDIENTS**

NOTES:

49

RECIPE:

| SERVES | PREPARATION TIME | COOK TIME | DATE |

DIRECTIONS

INGREDIENTS

NOTES:

RECIPE:

| SERVES | PREPARATION TIME | COOK TIME | DATE |

DIRECTIONS

INGREDIENTS

NOTES:

RECIPE:

SERVES

PREPARATION TIME

COOK TIME

DATE

DIRECTIONS

INGREDIENTS

NOTES:

RECIPE:

| SERVES | PREPARATION TIME | COOK TIME | DATE |

DIRECTIONS

INGREDIENTS

NOTES:

RECIPE:

SERVES

PREPARATION TIME

COOK TIME

DATE

DIRECTIONS

INGREDIENTS

NOTES:

RECIPE:

| SERVES | PREPARATION TIME | COOK TIME | DATE |

DIRECTIONS

INGREDIENTS

NOTES:

RECIPE:

SERVES

PREPARATION TIME

COOK TIME

DATE

DIRECTIONS

INGREDIENTS

NOTES:

RECIPE:

SERVES | PREPARATION TIME | COOK TIME | DATE

DIRECTIONS

INGREDIENTS

NOTES:

57

RECIPE:

| SERVES | PREPARATION TIME | COOK TIME | DATE |

DIRECTIONS

INGREDIENTS

NOTES:

RECIPE:

SERVES

PREPARATION TIME

COOK TIME

DATE

DIRECTIONS

INGREDIENTS

NOTES:

RECIPE:

SERVES

PREPARATION TIME

COOK TIME

DATE

DIRECTIONS

INGREDIENTS

NOTES:

60

RECIPE:

SERVES | PREPARATION TIME | COOK TIME | DATE

DIRECTIONS | INGREDIENTS

NOTES:

61  RECIPE:

SERVES **PREPARATION TIME** **COOK TIME** **DATE**

DIRECTIONS

INGREDIENTS

NOTES:

RECIPE:

| SERVES | PREPARATION TIME | COOK TIME | DATE |

DIRECTIONS

INGREDIENTS

NOTES:

RECIPE:

SERVES

PREPARATION TIME

COOK TIME

DATE

DIRECTIONS

INGREDIENTS

NOTES:

RECIPE:

SERVES | PREPARATION TIME | COOK TIME | DATE

DIRECTIONS

INGREDIENTS

NOTES:

RECIPE:

| SERVES | PREPARATION TIME | COOK TIME | DATE |

DIRECTIONS

INGREDIENTS

NOTES:

RECIPE:

SERVES

PREPARATION TIME

COOK TIME

DATE

DIRECTIONS

INGREDIENTS

NOTES:

RECIPE:

SERVES

PREPARATION TIME

COOK TIME

DATE

DIRECTIONS

INGREDIENTS

NOTES:

RECIPE:

SERVES

PREPARATION TIME

COOK TIME

DATE

DIRECTIONS

INGREDIENTS

NOTES:

RECIPE:

SERVES

PREPARATION TIME

COOK TIME

DATE

DIRECTIONS

INGREDIENTS

NOTES:

RECIPE:

SERVES **PREPARATION TIME** **COOK TIME** **DATE**

DIRECTIONS

INGREDIENTS

NOTES:

RECIPE:

| SERVES | PREPARATION TIME | COOK TIME | DATE |

DIRECTIONS

INGREDIENTS

NOTES:

RECIPE:

SERVES

PREPARATION TIME

COOK TIME

DATE

DIRECTIONS

INGREDIENTS

NOTES:

73

RECIPE:

| SERVES | PREPARATION TIME | COOK TIME | DATE |

DIRECTIONS

INGREDIENTS

NOTES:

RECIPE:

SERVES

PREPARATION TIME

COOK TIME

DATE

DIRECTIONS

INGREDIENTS

NOTES:

RECIPE:

SERVES	PREPARATION TIME	COOK TIME	DATE

DIRECTIONS

INGREDIENTS

NOTES:

RECIPE:

SERVES

PREPARATION TIME

COOK TIME

DATE

DIRECTIONS

INGREDIENTS

NOTES:

RECIPE:

SERVES

PREPARATION TIME

COOK TIME

DATE

DIRECTIONS

INGREDIENTS

NOTES:

RECIPE:

| SERVES | PREPARATION TIME | COOK TIME | DATE |

DIRECTIONS

INGREDIENTS

NOTES:

RECIPE:

| SERVES | PREPARATION TIME | COOK TIME | DATE |

DIRECTIONS

INGREDIENTS

NOTES:

RECIPE:

SERVES

PREPARATION TIME

COOK TIME

DATE

DIRECTIONS

INGREDIENTS

NOTES:

RECIPE:

SERVES

PREPARATION TIME

COOK TIME

DATE

DIRECTIONS

INGREDIENTS

NOTES:

RECIPE:

SERVES

PREPARATION TIME

COOK TIME

DATE

DIRECTIONS

INGREDIENTS

NOTES:

RECIPE:

SERVES | PREPARATION TIME | COOK TIME | DATE

DIRECTIONS

INGREDIENTS

NOTES:

RECIPE:

SERVES | PREPARATION TIME | COOK TIME | DATE

DIRECTIONS

INGREDIENTS

NOTES:

RECIPE:

SERVES

PREPARATION TIME

COOK TIME

DATE

DIRECTIONS

INGREDIENTS

NOTES:

RECIPE:

SERVES

PREPARATION TIME

COOK TIME

DATE

DIRECTIONS

INGREDIENTS

NOTES:

RECIPE:

SERVES

PREPARATION TIME

COOK TIME

DATE

DIRECTIONS

INGREDIENTS

NOTES:

RECIPE:

SERVES

PREPARATION TIME

COOK TIME

DATE

DIRECTIONS

INGREDIENTS

NOTES:

89

RECIPE:

SERVES	PREPARATION TIME	COOK TIME	DATE

DIRECTIONS

INGREDIENTS

NOTES:

RECIPE:

SERVES

PREPARATION TIME

COOK TIME

DATE

DIRECTIONS

INGREDIENTS

NOTES:

RECIPE:

SERVES

PREPARATION TIME

COOK TIME

DATE

DIRECTIONS

INGREDIENTS

NOTES:

RECIPE:

| SERVES | PREPARATION TIME | COOK TIME | DATE |

DIRECTIONS

INGREDIENTS

NOTES:

RECIPE:

SERVES

PREPARATION TIME

COOK TIME

DATE

DIRECTIONS

INGREDIENTS

NOTES:

RECIPE:

SERVES

PREPARATION TIME

COOK TIME

DATE

DIRECTIONS

INGREDIENTS

NOTES:

95

RECIPE:

SERVES

PREPARATION TIME

COOK TIME

DATE

DIRECTIONS

INGREDIENTS

NOTES:

RECIPE:

SERVES

PREPARATION TIME

COOK TIME

DATE

DIRECTIONS

INGREDIENTS

NOTES:

97

RECIPE:

| SERVES | PREPARATION TIME | COOK TIME | DATE |

DIRECTIONS

INGREDIENTS

NOTES:

RECIPE:

| SERVES | PREPARATION TIME | COOK TIME | DATE |

DIRECTIONS

INGREDIENTS

NOTES:

99

RECIPE:

| SERVES | PREPARATION TIME | COOK TIME | DATE |

DIRECTIONS

INGREDIENTS

NOTES:

100  RECIPE:

SERVES | PREPARATION TIME | COOK TIME | DATE

DIRECTIONS

INGREDIENTS

NOTES:

www.ingramcontent.com/pod-product-compliance
Lightning Source LLC
Chambersburg PA
CBHW081430070526
44586CB00020B/2546